The Thinking Tree

Queens, Brides & Divas
WOMEN OF THE BIBLE
A Poet's Devotional
& Prayer Journal

Anna Miriam Brown

Sarah Janisse Brown

About Women of the Bible

This journal is a study of ten important women of the Bible, from Eve to Mary Magdalene. It includes poems, prayers, and biblical verses about their lives and invites you to do additional research and write your own prayers as you reflect and spend quiet time in worship. Finally, you can record what you've learned from them and how to apply this to your own life.

Eve

Come Find Me

We walked and talked
in the cool of the day
God told me of His dreams
Of communion and peace
With the world He made
To rest by quiet streams

To enjoy the presence of our Maker
To make each moment count
To thrive on nature
and the voice of our Creator
And the well that never runs out

All seemed almost perfect
Till I caught a stranger's eye
He said the one tree God forbade us
Was the one we had to try

He went on of its glories
I explained that we would die
"Just take a bite, just trust me,
God knows it will make you wise"

"All at once you'll be like Him"
And so it was that way
I took a bite and all at once
My eyes opened to my shame

My heart was broken I was lost
I ran and tried to hide
But you can't hide from yourself
Or the feeling you have died

My soul was torn from His
Our image torn apart
If God finds out what I did
It will surely break His heart

I heard my Maker's footsteps
I heard my Maker speak
He sadly asked "Where are you?"
I felt my soul grow weak

It was a question for creation
In His voice I heard His grief
As well as grace, I could call back
And say,
"I'm here. Come find me, please!"

.Eve

When she walked away...

He came to find her...

Prayer...

In all of our lives there have been times we've walked away from our Maker, but the beautiful thing is, at any second, we can call out "I'm here, come find me please," And our Savior will rush to our side.

Use this page to write a prayer of thankfulness to the wonderful God who is always there, asking us where we are, just waiting for us to call Him to come save us.

_____
_____
_____
_____
_____
_____
_____
_____
_____
_____
_____
_____
_____
_____
_____
_____
_____

Adam named his wife Eve,
because she would become
the mother of all the living.

Genesis 3:20

What can we learn from Eve?

_____

_____

_____

_____

_____

_____

_____

_____

_____

_____

_____

_____

_____

_____

_____

_____

What's on your mind?

Mother Of Moses

Don't Cry

Little Moses, this is your last hope
Please don't cry, son, be quiet
My baby boy, you must go
I beg our Lord you survive this

In these times we live as slaves
The scars on our backs
May outnumber our days
But you have a chance, son, be brave
And come back to save us one day

So I'm giving you a fighting chance
The hardest thing a mother can do
Is let her child let go of her hand
I don't wanna let go of you

So I pray Yahweh will bring you home
Come save us when you survive this
Little Moses you're our last hope
Please don't cry, son, be quiet

.Mother Of Moses

When She trusted He would save her...

He did..

Prayer...

Just like the mother of Moses,

We all have had times we have to trust.

To just launch what matters most to us,

Into the fierce waves with only a prayer protecting it.

Take this page to give God what matters most to you.

What's aching your heart?

What do you long for? What terrifies you?

Give it to God and watch Him do beyond all you ever expected.

_____

_____

_____

_____

_____

_____

_____

_____

_____

_____

_____

_____

_____

_____

_____

_____

But when she could hide him no
longer, she got a papyrus basket for
him and coated it with tar and pitch.
Then she placed the child in it and
put it among the reeds along the
bank of the Nile.

Exodus 2:3

What can we learn

from the Mother of Moses?

What's on your mind?

Delilah

At All

Pursuing purpose in all the wrong places
I'll flirt and I'll flatter with faces and phases
Little looks got em' hooked, can't resist when I say it
Come join me in my oasis

Little whispers turn to bigger lies
The secret of his weakness remained in his eyes
So I took him by surprise, he couldn't keep his secret
His beautiful hair was his weakness

So one night after I watched him fall asleep
I cut off his hair and watched him grow weak
Sold him away, for a price was agreed
He was blinded and broken and beat

His enemies threw a party, chained him to the wall,
We celebrated our rise and laughed at his fall
All of us froze and watched Samson cry
"Lord, give me strength one last time"

The ceiling crumbled, we watched the walls crack
All at once my life came to me in flash
Asking myself was the rise worth the fall
No, it wasn't worth it at all

.Delilah

If she asked for forgiveness..

He would've forgiven her...

Prayer...

We've all made mistakes.

But it's not about the mistakes,

It's about what you do when you see you've messed up.

Do you turn to the world?

Or do you turn to God?

Take this page to pray for God to make you new

And be the strength in your weakness.

_____

_____

_____

_____

_____

_____

_____

_____

_____

_____

_____

_____

_____

_____

Some time later, he fell in love with a woman in the Valley of Sorek whose name was Delilah. The rulers of the Philistines went to her and said, "See if you can lure him into showing you the secret of his great strength and how we can overpower him so we may tie him up and subdue him. Each one of us will give you eleven hundred shekels of silver."

Judges 16:4-5

What can we learn from Delilah?

_____

_____

_____

_____

_____

_____

_____

_____

_____

_____

_____

_____

_____

_____

_____

_____

_____

_____

What's on your mind?

Ruth

To Heal

We all have known the darkness
What seems eternal night
But will you choose to dwell in darkness
Or go searching for the light

I found myself alone once
The one I loved had died
As broken as I was
I looked up to sky

I knew my God would see me
Though pain is all I've known
I knew He'd never leave me
I knew He'd lead me home

Lead me to a safer place
A place where grace abounds
With a smile on my face
where love and faith abound
We all have known the darkness
And though the pain is real
Will you choose to keep the darkness
Or find a way to heal

Ruth

When she was in pain...

He became her healer...

Prayer...

Like Ruth, we've all had pain.

But with every night there is a sunrise.

Take this page to give your pain to God and let Him heal you.

_____

_____

_____

_____

_____

_____

_____

_____

_____

_____

_____

_____

_____

_____

_____

"The Lord bless you, my daughter," he replied. "This kindness is greater than that which you showed earlier: You have not run after the younger men, whether rich or poor. And now, my daughter, don't be afraid. I will do for you all you ask. All the people of my town know that you are a woman of noble character."

Ruth 3:10-11

What can we learn from Ruth?

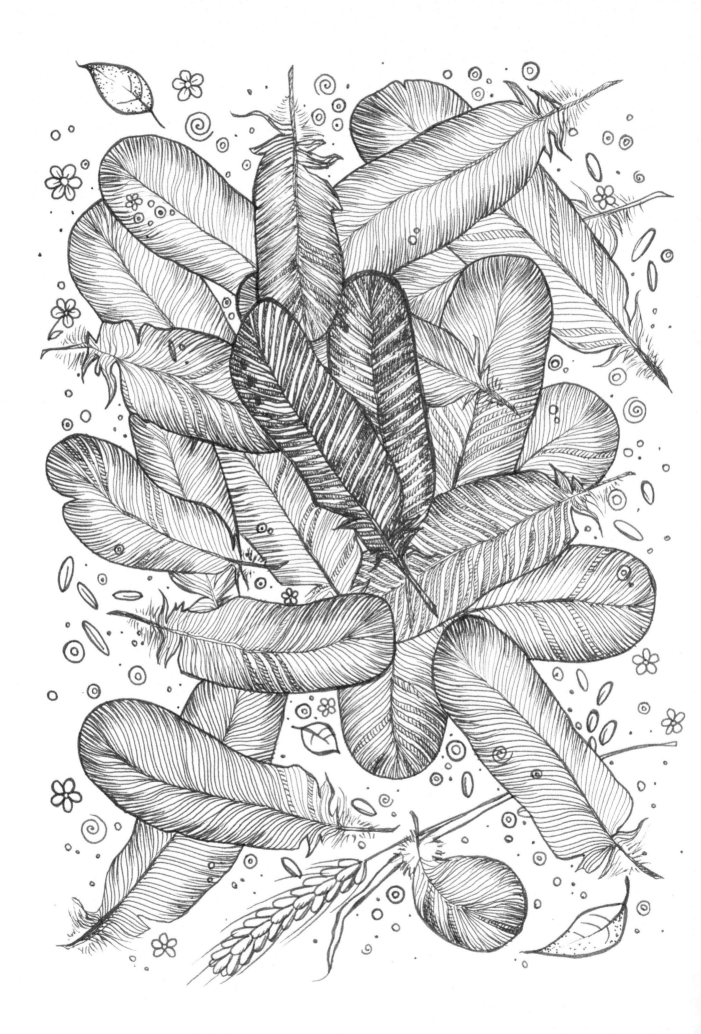

What's on your mind?

Bathsheba

Show Me How

Glimpses of eternity
I know that I have seen them
Cause when Your people smile
They smile for a reason
David says we're incomplete
Well I'm searching for completion
But I don't know how to
Love you in my weakness

If You offer me a new one
I'll throw away my old heart
If You show me how to love You
I'll love You with my whole heart
But I'm not good at loving
As sorrow seems to seek me
But I'd be willing to learn, Lord
If You'd be willing to teach me

Through sorrow I still see Your grace
As I look on to my son
As I look at Solomon's smiling face
And I see all that You've done

Even through the sting of death
You've promised me Your plan
You've promised that my baby's safe
I have faith he's in Your hands

I feel as if I can't do enough
I'm not enough for You
I don't know how to love
Lord what else can I do?

Lord, please hear my prayer
Lord, please, what can I do?
Then he whispered in my ear
"Be still, let me love you"
                    -Bathsheba

In her time of doubt...

He showed Himself...

Prayer...

I think we've all had times of doubt.

We know God is real and we know He loves us.

But it seems so hard to understand.

Why would God love me?

We feel like we never have enough faith,

Love and devotion to deserve His love,

Take this page to let God love you, thank Him for His faithful,

Unrelenting love for you even when you're in doubt.

_____

_____

_____

_____

_____

_____

_____

_____

_____

_____

_____

_____

_____

_____

_____

Then David comforted his wife Bathsheba, and went in to her and lay with her; and she gave birth to a son, and he named him Solomon. Now the LORD loved him.

2 Samuel 12:24

What can we learn from Bathsheba?

_____

_____

_____

_____

_____

_____

_____

_____

_____

_____

_____

_____

_____

_____

_____

_____

_____

What's on your mind?

Esther

From This Moment

Maybe I was made for this moment
And just maybe I'm mistaken
But I look at their faces, they're hopeless
So they'll die or I'll rise to the occasion

A nation prays as they brace themselves
It seems there's no hope prayer can bring
So I must be brave and face myself
Face my fears as I'm facing my king

God put me here, that I know
I think back on sweet moments I've cherished
So as their sister and queen I won't leave them alone
If I perish, I perish

Maybe I was made for this moment
And still I may be mistaken
But I look in the mirror, there's hope
a warrior the Lord has awakened

A warrior draped in precious stones
Their burden, but I'll choose to bear it
As your queen and your sister I'll go
And If I perish, I perish
-Esther

When she needed bravery...

He gave her Himself...

Prayer...

Bravery.

Bravery isn't the lack of fear, but action in the midst of it.

We have all faced fear and life won't let us go through it without

Stumbling on frightening moments now and then.

Take this page to ask God for bravery.

Ask Him to use you,

To change the world in a way you could never imagine.

Look in the Bible. God doesn't base His anointing on who we are

But who He knows we can be with His help.

The only thing you must be is willing.

He will take care of the rest.

_____

_____

_____

_____

_____

_____

_____

_____

_____

_____

_____

_____

"Go, gather together all the Jews who are in Susa, and fast for me. Do not eat or drink for three days, night or day. I and my attendants will fast as you do. When this is done, I will go to the king, even though it is against the law.
And if I perish, I perish."

Esther 4:16

What can we learn from Esther?

_____

_____

_____

_____

_____

_____

_____

_____

_____

_____

_____

_____

_____

_____

_____

_____

_____

_____

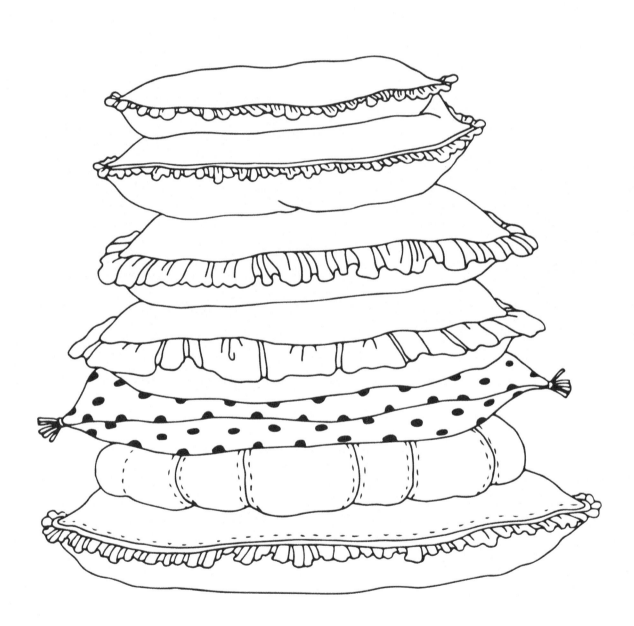

What's on your mind?

Mary

Arriving

The time is coming soon
for my baby to arrive
I cannot wait to hold You
To look You in the eyes

My baby You should know
That your mama's by Your side
As I watch You change the world
I'll stand by You with pride

"My Son's the Son of God."
I didn't know the meaning
Till I saw You hanging on a cross
And both our hearts stopped beating

What kind of mother was I
To let my Son be beat
Till I realized His beatings
Would heal eternity

I take a breath and step back
From my baby in the manger
He wasn't just my Son
He would one day be my Savior

-Mary

She had to let go...

To let Him hold her...

Prayer...

What grace the Father had on us to send His own Son to die!

People so often say that Jesus died for our sins,

But that is an understatement.

Jesus died for us, not just sinners, but lost sons and daughters. He

died because He saw us as worth it. He wanted us free,

Free to leave sin, free to live life abundantly,

And above all, Free to know Him.

Not just as a Lord and Savior but a close friend.

Take this page to thank Jesus for what He did

Just to bring us to Himself.

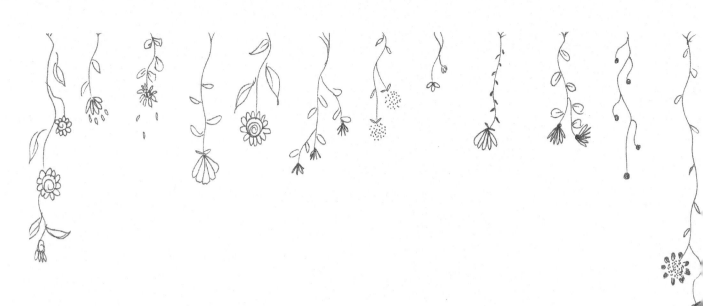

The angel answered her, "The Holy Spirit will come to you, and the power of the Most High will overshadow you. Therefore, the holy child developing inside you will be called the Son of God."

Luke 1:35

What can we learn from Mary?

_____

_____

_____

_____

_____

_____

_____

_____

_____

_____

_____

_____

_____

_____

_____

What's on your mind?

The Adulteress

You are Free

They pulled me out into the streets
My shame there in the open
My lover left and left me
Helplessly naked and broken

Why must I be so careless
Why couldn't I say no
I took the luxury of his lust
Where I should've
turned to go

I saw my life before my eyes
A life had gone to waste
Till Life Himself,
To my surprise
Bent down to see my face

Crowds went still
and held their stones
As condemnation reversed
Then with grace my Savior spoke
"If you've never sinned
Throw at her first."

I heard stones hit the ground
I heard my Maker speak
"I don't condemn you either,
Go sin no more, you're free."

They pulled him up onto a cross
His shame there in the open
Sin weighed on the Son of God
Bittersweetly beat and broken

I questioned who had done this
Then broke, cause it was me
With dying breath, His eyes spoke
"Go sin no more, you're free."
-The Adulteress

When she was condemned...

He was grace...

Prayer...

Without His grace we are condemned.

But there is grace.

Jesus walks into the scene and changes everything.

He sets her free and releases her from her sins,

Sends away her accusers and makes her clean.

We see this story and are amazed,

But I'm not sure we fully realize what Jesus has done.

He smiled as she walked away shameless and sinless,

But we don't instantly realize what He did.

He put her sin on Himself, knowing full well He will be taking her punishment later.

Beaten and killed for her freedom.

We can be just like her, living our life in complete freedom not fully realizing that

2000 years ago Jesus took whips and beatings to give us such freedom.

Through the tears and blood He pictured us free and decided we were worth it.

Take this page to thank Jesus for that.

_____

_____

_____

_____

_____

_____

_____

_____

Then Jesus straightened up
and asked her, "Woman, where
are your accusers? Has no one
condemned you?"

"No one, Lord," she answered.

"Then neither do I condemn
you," Jesus declared.

"Now go and sin no more."

John 8:10-11

What can we learn from the adulteress?

_____

_____

_____

_____

_____

_____

_____

_____

_____

_____

_____

_____

_____

_____

_____

_____

_____

What's on your mind?

Martha

Come, Rest

"Come rest, my burden is light."
I hear my Teacher teach
With tired hands and heavy eyes
I see His eyes on me

Were His words for me?
I wasn't sure until
He said, "come to my feet,
Just listen, just be still."

I couldn't believe my own ears
As I brush my dirty skirt
"No, Master, let me serve You."
"I came to serve, not to be served."

This thing called faith is new to me
Unsure, I must confess
It seemed odd, that God, the Maker
Would call His own to rest

So I slowly sit down at His feet
Relieved, at peace, and still
The Son of God told me to rest
So no doubt, rest I will

-Martha

When she wanted to serve Him..

He asked her to sit at His feet..

Prayer...

So often we forget to just come and rest.

To show up at His feet and listen to Him talk.

To let Him heal us, to come to know Him just to know Him,

Not to just check a checkmark off our daily routine.

If you feel this can be you sometimes,

Take this page to repent and refocus.

Ask Jesus to change your perspective.

_____

_____

_____

_____

_____

_____

_____

_____

_____

_____

_____

_____

And Jesus answered
and said to her, "Martha, Martha,
you are worried and troubled
about many things. But one thing
is needed, and Mary has chosen
that good part, which will not be
taken away from her."

Luke 10:41-42

What can we learn from Martha?

_____

_____

_____

_____

_____

_____

_____

_____

_____

_____

_____

_____

_____

_____

_____

_____

What's on your mind?

Mary Magdalene

To Be Enough

I didn't have it in me to change
Cause evil made home in my soul
All the men knew me by name
My future beyond my control

I did what I did to survive
I was lost and hope was dim
Till I met eyes with a stranger

Who came to be my Savior
And He told me what I meant to Him

He called me with a gentle voice
He spoke evil away
All at once my soul was full of joy
And the pain began to fade

He said there was a future for me
When I was just a girl
He looked down at little Miss Magdalene and said,
"One day she'll change the world"

I didn't have it in me to change
But then again, who does?
Jesus taught me it's ok
We were never supposed to be enough

-Mary Magdalene

When she wasn't enough...

He was.

Prayer...

It's so easy to feel unworthy.

So much of my walk with God was spent trying to be enough

To have enough faith and be a perfect Christian.

Someone worthy of grace.

But one day my head was flooded with questions and doubt

I was frustrated with myself. I couldn't do it. I couldn't believe enough.

My faith felt weak.

There was no way faith like that could get me to heaven.

I told God, "I can't do it, I can't believe."

"My faith is not enough. I'm not enough."

And God spoke to my heart and calmed the storm in my soul

With seven words. "You were never supposed to be enough."

Then it all made sense.

The whole point of grace.

We can never be enough but He is.

That's the gospel.

Take this time to thank Jesus for being enough. Because He is.

_____

_____

_____

_____

_____

_____

Jesus said to her, "Mary."

She turned and said to him in

Aramaic, "Rabboni!"

(which means Teacher).

John 20:16

What can we learn from Miss Magdalene?

What's on your mind?

Fun-Schooling With Thinking Tree Books

Contact Us:

Thinking Tree LLC
+1 (USA)   317.622.8852

info@funschooling.com

THE THINKING TREE

FunSchooling.com

Made in the USA
Coppell, TX
06 February 2023

12305083R00050